Kefalonia
Travel Guide

Quick Trips Series

No part of this publication may be reproduced, stored in a retrieval system, or transmitted, in any form or by any means without the prior written permission of the publisher, nor be otherwise circulated in any form of binding or cover other than that in which it is published and without similar condition being imposed on the subsequent purchaser. If there are any errors or omissions in copyright acknowledgements the publisher will be pleased to insert the appropriate acknowledgement in any subsequent printing of this publication. Although we have taken all reasonable care in researching this book we make no warranty about the accuracy or completeness of its content and disclaim all liability arising from its use.

Copyright © 2016, Astute Press
All Rights Reserved.

Table of Contents

KEFALONIA 6
- 🌐 CUSTOMS & CULTURE 11
- 🌐 GEOGRAPHY 15
- 🌐 WEATHER & BEST TIME TO VISIT 16

SIGHTS & ACTIVITIES: WHAT TO SEE & DO 20
- 🌐 ARCHAEOLOGICAL MUSEUM OF ARGOSTOLI (KEFALONIA MUSEUM) 20
- 🌐 MELISSANI CAVE 22
- 🌐 GLASS BOTTOM BOAT TOUR 23
- 🌐 DROGARATI CAVE 25
- 🌐 ARGOSTOLI LIGHTHOUSE & KATAVOTHRES 26
  - Argostoli Lighthouse 26
  - Katavothres 27
- 🌐 MONASTERY OF KIPOUREON 28
- 🌐 CASTLE OF SAINT GEORGE 30
- 🌐 HISTORY & FOLKLORE MUSEUM OF ARGOSTOLI 31
- 🌐 KOUTAVOS LAGOON 32
- 🌐 THREE ISLAND CRUISE 34
- 🌐 SKALA BEACH & TOWN 35

BUDGET TIPS 38
- 🌐 ACCOMMODATION 38

Asta la Vista Mezonetes by the Sea..38
Dioni Studios & Apartments 39
Alexatos Studios & Apartments 40
Star Villas Apartments..41
Ventura Rooms 42

⊕ Restaurants, Cafés & Bars 43
Acropolis..43
Kaliva...44
Taverna To Pefko 45
Polyphemus..46
Tselentis...47

⊕ Shopping 48
Down the Rabbit Hole 49
Pantazatos Supermarket & Delicatessen 49
Robola Cooperative Factory Shop..50
G G Garbis...51
Olive Press Gift Shop 52

KNOW BEFORE YOU GO   54

⊕ Entry Requirements 54
⊕ Health Insurance..55
⊕ Travelling with Pets...55
⊕ Airports 56
⊕ Airlines 57
⊕ Currency...58
⊕ Banking & ATMs 58
⊕ Credit Cards 59
⊕ Reclaiming VAT 59
⊕ Tipping Policy 60
⊕ Mobile Phones 61
⊕ Dialling Code 62

- Emergency numbers 62
- Public Holidays 62
- Time Zone 63
- Daylight Savings Time 63
- School Holidays 64
- Trading Hours 64
- Driving Laws 64
- Smoking Laws 65
- Drinking Laws 66
- Electricity 66
- Tourist Information (TI) 66
- Food & Drink 67
- Websites 68

KEFALONIA TRAVEL GUIDE

Kefalonia

Kefalonia is the largest of the Ionian Islands and the sixth largest of the Greek Islands. It offers dramatic scenery and attracts the more discerning holidaymaker.

Kefalonia's picturesque inlets and bays have carved its unusual shape. The island's northern coastline features pebbled beaches and rugged cliffs while in the south long stretches of sand attract sunshine and beach lovers.

KEFALONIA TRAVEL GUIDE

The roads have good access for car travel and travelling by foot, horse and bicycle is often possible and is a rewarding way to discover the island. The islands of Ithaca, Zante and Lefkas are close enough to visit by ferry on a day trip.

In the world scenic beauty league Kefalonia was voted 10th and it is easy to why. There is plenty to see and do with over 200 villages hidden away in olive groves and wooded valleys. There are underground lakes and caves waiting to be visited as well as castles, monasteries and churches.

Kefalonia is a fantastic place to laze on beautiful beaches where the turquoise sea shimmers under the

KEFALONIA TRAVEL GUIDE

Mediterranean sun. As yet undiscovered by mass tourism and lager louts it is the ideal place to chill out and relax.

The fishing villages of Lixouri and Argostoli are the main fishing centres and the local waters are teeming with fish wherever you go.

Kefalonia has been inhabited since the Paleolithic era and owes its name to the first king of the island, Kephalos. He founded the four main towns of the island, Krani, Sami, Pronnoi and Pahli, naming them after his four sons. Each town had its own coins and rules.

Kefalonia might be small but it was highly desirable and fought over and ruled by many different people. After the Peloponnesian and Persian Wars the Romans took possession of the island in 187BC and turned Kefalonia

KEFALONIA TRAVEL GUIDE

into a naval base but the island still suffered from raids by pirates and other invaders.

Through mediaeval times the danger came from the Saracens and by the 11th century it was the end of an era as Kefalonia was conquered by the Normans, Orsinis, Andeans and Toscans. By 1480 the Turkish had attacked this tiny island but they just devastated it and then deserted it. By now the Venetians and Spanish had taken over.

In 1757 much of the island was destroyed by an earthquake, many locals simply gave up on their homeland and left to search for a better life. The capital moved to Argostoli where it remains today. Dominated by the Venetians the island has three distinct social classes

KEFALONIA TRAVEL GUIDE

but this was ended in 1795 when the French arrived and chased away the Venetians.

The French rule didn't last long and they were soon defeated by Turks, Russians and English. By 1809 Kefalonia was under British rule, this lasted until 1864 when with the rest of the Ionian Islands it became united with Greece.

In WWII Italian troops occupied the island, which had a sad ending when 5,000 soldiers were killed by the Nazis. This part of Kefalonia's history is described in the book by Louis de Bernieres; Captain Corelli's Mandolin.

In more recent times Kefalonia suffered almost total devastation in the earthquake of 1953 and the only village untouched was the fishing port of Fiskardo. Nowadays

KEFALONIA TRAVEL GUIDE

Fiskardo is very popular with visitors and the 18th century houses cluster around the L-shaped harbour.

There is a wide selection of shady tavernas to have a meal and relax in and watch the fishermen at work in their brightly painted boats.

For beach lovers there is a wide choice but Myrtos beach has to be the most jaw-droppingly beautiful. The fine white sand is lapped by the crystal clear sea which makes swimming and snorkelling a pleasure. There is a small taverna for drinks and snacks or take a picnic. Access is by a very steep road or you can book boat trips from many of the small towns and villages.

The main shopping area in Kefalonia is the capital town of Argostoli. The more traditional products to look for are

KEFALONIA TRAVEL GUIDE

ceramics, honey and local wine, as well as exclusive ranges of jewellery, leather, clothes and shoes. The town of Lixouri is just across the bay from Argostoli and was almost totally destroyed which is why most of the buildings there are of recent construction.

For eating out the meze is a great way to try a variety of Greek dishes all at once. The meze consists of plates of local meat and fish dishes as well as small plates of dips which are all shared. Nightlife is fairly low-key on this peaceful island but there are nightclubs in the bigger resorts. One of the treats of the island and not to be missed it the delicious feta cheese made from ewes and goats milk as well as many other succulent cheeses.

KEFALONIA TRAVEL GUIDE

🌍 Customs & Culture

The inhabitants of Kefalonia need very little excuse to party! The Greeks are a hospitable people and the locals welcome tourists with their friendly attitude. Just remember a few simple rules of etiquette. Nudity is frowned upon on most of the beaches and the more traditional Greeks find it very offensive, particularly if the beach is near to a church. While the Greeks love to party and make lots of noise the equivalent to the Spanish siesta 'mikro ipno' is still widely observed between 3pm and 5pm when peace and quiet is appreciated.

Family ties are very strong throughout the islands and the elders are greatly respected. Any disrespect to the Greek Orthodox Church or Greek state is frowned upon and verbal insults are punishable by court action. Photography

KEFALONIA TRAVEL GUIDE

near military areas is strictly forbidden and can also land you in jail.

While visiting Kefalonia you might hear the characteristic songs of the region called Kantades. The words are Greek although the music has Italian influences and they are sung by men with very deep voices. Roughly translated as serenade these musical greetings are usually performed outside in the evenings between friends and lovers. Another traditional song, the Arietta, is sung by the fishermen of Lixouri. Unaccompanied by music the songs are sung by a quartet of men where one starts the song and the rest follow him.

For theatregoers and lovers of music, drama and films there are two air-conditioned and modern theatres on Kefalonia. There is one in Lixouri and one in Argostoli

KEFALONIA TRAVEL GUIDE

both offering varied programmes all the year round as well as an open air cinema in Argostoli in the summer.

There are many festivals and events that take place on the island throughout the year. The most important of these is the feast day of Saint Gerasimos, the patron saint of Kefalonia. On the 15th and 16th August at the monastery in the Omala valley an all-night vigil is held with a church service and procession the following day. There is a two day traditional market and the area is full to bursting point as tourists and pilgrims alike come to pay their respects.

Other festivals include the Robola Wine Festival and the International Music Festival of Argostoli which are both held in August. The biggest and noisiest festival is the Kefalonia Carnival in Argostoli also held in August. This is

KEFALONIA TRAVEL GUIDE

a great time to join in the parades and partying, singing and dancing in a fun-filled atmosphere along with locals. A fancy dress procession winds its way through Argostoli ending up by the Archaeological Museum where the judges wait to award prizes to the best costume. A prize of around €400 goes to the winner.

One of the more unusual traditions on Kefalonia happens on the slopes of Mount Ainos which stands at just over five thousand feet and is home to a beautiful natural park. Markopoulo, population 90, is a tiny village clinging to the side of the mountain and is unvisited by tourists for most of the year. On 15th August every year the Snake Festival is held and the village is swamped as locals and visitors come to see this unusual ritual.

KEFALONIA TRAVEL GUIDE

According to legend the convent at Markopoulo was going to be attacked by pirates. The nuns prayed to the Virgin Mary for help and were turned into small snakes so they could hide. Every year on the same date the snakes return and ascend the bell tower of the church. If the snakes fail to appear it is seen as a bad omen. The last times that they didn't show themselves was the year of the 1953 earthquake and the year of the Axis powers occupation!

🌍 Geography

The island of Kefalonia is quite small at only 25 by 20 miles. It is located about 175 miles from Athens. The population is around 40,000 of which 98% are Greek Orthodox, with Muslim, Roman Catholic and Jewish minorities.

KEFALONIA TRAVEL GUIDE

The main crop on the island is olives; there are over one million olive trees, with other parts of island dedicated to grapevines and orange trees. Tourism now plays an important part in the economy of the island as does fishing.

To get to Kefalonia you can fly into the small airport near Svoronata in the south of the island. Argostoli is about 25 minutes from the airport but nowhere is more than a couple of hours away. Most of the flights to Kefalonia are scheduled services from Athens with Olympic Air and a number of charter flights visit throughout the summer months.

There are several harbours and ports on Kefalonia, Argostoli has the largest port and there are regular ferries and local boats to Zante and Lixouri. The ferry from

Argostoli to Lixouri is a popular way of getting between the two towns and the ferry ride across the bay is only two miles instead of ten times that distance by road. From Sami there are boat links to Ithaca. From Poros in the south you can take the ferry to Kyllini and in the north Fiskardo has ferries to Ithaca and Lefkas.

The roads are good and mainly asphalt and car hire is recommended to get to the more remote parts of the island. Bus services are limited with only two departures a day to some of the more rural areas.

🌍 Weather & Best Time to Visit

The climate on Kefalonia promises long, hot, dry summers with rainy winters and the average rainfall can be as much as three times that of the Aegean Islands.

KEFALONIA TRAVEL GUIDE

This gives the island its many forests with lush vegetation as well fertile plains for agriculture.

Spring temperatures can be from lows of 9°C to highs of 24°C as the summer months approach. There are several hours of sunshine and with such pleasant weather this is an ideal season for walking and sightseeing. If anyone is feeling brave the sea will be warm if you fancy a dip!

The temperatures in summer can reach 30°C with at least 12 hours of sunshine a day. The summer weather is reliable and for sun lovers Kefalonia is a great place for a beach holiday. There are little or no winds through the summer months to spoil the warm weather so make sure you are armed with suntan cream and plenty of water. Even at night the mercury rarely falls lower than 18°C.

KEFALONIA TRAVEL GUIDE

Rain returns in the autumn although Kefalonia is still relatively warm and there are lots of sunshine hours. The temperatures usually beat the springtime with highs of 28°C and a low of 12 °C. Daytime id still nice enough to be out and about in short sleeves but the nights will be cooler as winter approaches.

Winter is quite pleasant, frost or snow is rare as the temperatures rarely falls below 7°C. In the daytime 14°C can be seen if you're lucky. It does get wetter in the winter months with the rain helping to keep the island looking lush and verdant. Like many Mediterranean islands, Kefalonia is mostly equipped for the sunny high season, and in the winter it can be a bit quiet. No heating or carpets means that thick socks and a good duvet at night are essential.

KEFALONIA TRAVEL GUIDE

Kefalonia is prone to earthquakes caused by three tectonic plates close to the island, and it neighbours Zante and Ithaca. The 1953 earthquake was the most devastating when much of the island was razed to the ground. In 2003 the Lefkada quake shook the island but little damage was seen. Three months later a similar quake caused some structural damage around Argostoli.

In the autumn of 2005 Lixouri residents were shaken awake when an early morning quake measured 4.9 on the Richter scale. Several months later in January a major snowstorm hit the island causing power failures and disruption.

More recently in January and February 2014 a powerful earthquake caused widespread damage and left many people homeless as buildings collapsed.

KEFALONIA TRAVEL GUIDE

Sights & Activities: What to See & Do

🌍 Archaeological Museum of Argostoli (Kefalonia Museum)

Γ. Βεργωτή

G. Vergoti street

Argostoli 28100

Kefalonia

Tel: +30 2671 028300

KEFALONIA TRAVEL GUIDE

www.leepka.gr/

This museum is located not far from the Municipal Theatre and was rebuilt in 1960 after the original one was destroyed in the 1953 earthquake.

There are extensive collections of artefacts from the Mycenaean period and antiquities from prehistoric to Roman times. One of the most valuable pieces is the 'kylix' a 12th century conical cup unearthed at Lakithra Cemetery. When Melissani Lake was excavated many items were discovered; there are several pieces depicting nymphs as well as a clay figure of Pan.

The opening hours are Tuesday to Sunday from 8.30am to 3pm and the entrance fee is €3

🌍 Melissani Cave

Aghia Efimia

Sami / Karavomilo

Kefalonia

The cave and lake are surrounded by lush forests but car access is possible and there is a large car park. In mythology this was the cave of the nymphs and the sky blue lake with pretty stones at the bottom is a very popular tourist spot. Legend tells us that the nymph Melissanthi committed suicide and fell in the water when Pan did not reciprocate her feelings.

The lake was rediscovered in 1951 by speleontologist Giannis Petrocheilos but was changed forever in the 1953 earthquake when the roof caved in leaving the opening that exists today.

KEFALONIA TRAVEL GUIDE

The cave itself covers a couple of miles underground and rises to a height of about 120 feet with amazing and unusual rock formations and structures. The Hydrogeology of the Melissani Cave is fascinating and has been explored by many divers. The water is a mixture of sea water and fresh water which is very unusual.

A small boat will take you on a magical ride through the tunnel until you come out on the lake, now open to the beautiful blue sky. Take a boat ride at the right time when the sun is beaming down through the opening and the lake sparkles with incredibly blue brilliance.

The cave and lake are open from Easter until October and there is an entry fee of about €5 per adult, children half-price, to access the tunnel and lake. The boat rides cost around €4 per person extra and lasts 15 minutes. There is a café, gift shop and toilets at the entrance.

 Glass Bottom Boat Tour

Suncruise

Argostoli Harbour

Kefalonia

Tel: +30 2671 025775

www.users.otenet.gr/~mafokas/

Captain Makis Fokas has been running tours on Kefalonia for many years with his Suncruise Glass Bottom Boat. The boat departs from Argostoli harbour and portholes below sea level mean you can view the beautiful marine life swimming in the clear blue sea.

KEFALONIA TRAVEL GUIDE

The cruise takes a route of fish farms, local shipwrecks and then on to Vardiani island for swimming and snorkelling in the crystal clear water. Next stop is the red sands of Xi beach for a BBQ with unlimited local wine and souvlaki.

After lunch there is time to have a mud bath at the local clay cliffs before having a relaxing sail back to Argostoli in time for dinner. This is an all day tour from 9am to 5.30 pm on Wednesday, Thursday and Saturday. Adults pay €50 and children €35.

🌑 Drogarati Cave

Ionia Nisia, 28080

Kefalonia

Tel.: +30 2674 023302

KEFALONIA TRAVEL GUIDE

The Drogarati Cave is 150 million years old and is one of nature's dramatic works of art. Even the earthquakes haven't destroyed the beauty of the underground chamber where beautiful stalactites hang down growing imperceptibly day by day.

Part of the cave is accessible to visitors and is often used for cultural performances. An audience of up to 500 can be seated in the Chamber of Exultation with its amazing acoustics to watch the musicians on the natural stage. Visitors can walk through the tunnel to the Royal Balcony where the glittering stalactites reflect the light in a dazzling display.

The temperature in the cave remains at a constant 18°C all year round and the oxygen supply is more than adequate.

KEFALONIA TRAVEL GUIDE

Drogarati Cave is open every day from 8am to 8pm and the entrance fee is €5. There are a lot of steps so it might not be suitable for people with limited mobility.

🌐 Argostoli Lighthouse & Katavothres

For a pleasant walk around the inviting shores of Kefalonia take the coastal path off the Argostoli main road at the north end towards Lassi. Follow the path round the headland, past the lighthouse and carry on towards the Katavothres water wheel.

Argostoli Lighthouse

Lassi

Kefalonia

The lighthouse was built in 1829 and then rebuilt again after the 1875 earthquake. It is still operational and keeps boats approaching the Argostoli harbour way from the treacherous rocks. There is a small car park at the lighthouse if you prefer to drive.

There are beautiful views back towards Argostoli and across the water to Lixouri and you might catch a glimpse of the ferries going backwards and forwards between these two towns and Killini.

Katavothres

Agios Theodoros

Kefalonia

Half a mile further round the coast is the water wheel of Katavothres where there is a very pleasant bar for a refreshing drink and a sit down. There is a lovely promenade with far-reaching views across the sea and other parts of the island.

The water wheel was built by an Englishman, Stevens, in 1835 when he realised the potential of water as a power source, it is no longer operational but makes a great tourist attraction.

What are more fascinating than the wheel itself are the openings in the ground by the sea or sinks. The island is made up of Karst rock so the water runs in through the sinks and via the subterranean network of channels and tunnels comes out at various points across the island.

The paths run for several miles underground and this was proven by two geologists who dropped several gallons of dye into the sinks. Traces of the dye appeared two weeks later about ten miles away as well as in the lake at the Melissani Cave.

Monastery of Kipoureon

Χερσόνησος της Παλικής

Lixouri 28200

Kefalonia

Tel: +30 2671 091354

Some of the most breathtaking scenery on the island can be seen from this monastery close to Lixouri. Perched high above the sea the views of the rugged coastline and Ionian Sea really are spectacular.

Founded in the 17th century this once thriving monastery had 80 monks tending the gardens but is now only home to just one. He welcomes visitors every day to the beautiful gardens and to sit with him in the inner courtyard or to watch the spectacular sunsets.

Inside the monastery are some intricate and interesting relics from various saints and the miraculous icon of Saint Paraskevi which was the sole survivor of the devastated Taphion monastery. The Kipoureon monastery is dedicated to the Annunciation of the Virgin Mary and there is a quite miraculous picture of her to admire along with dazzling chandeliers and ornate décor.

🌎 Castle of Saint George

Agios Georgios

Kefalonia

On a peak of a thousand feet above the villages of

KEFALONIA TRAVEL GUIDE

Travilata and Peratata sits this very impressive castle. Dating from the 11th century the location offers panoramic views in all directions and was ideal for the 15,000 residents to keep a watch out for any attacking pirates or invading marauders.

Completed eventually in 1545 the surrounding wall runs for several hundred feet and encloses a vast area. The courtyard is horseshoe shaped and built around a central tower and throughout the castle there are coats of arms from various Venetian families.

There is a café and taverna nearby in the old capital town of Agios Georgios aka Kastro as well as a gift shop selling ceramics and paintings and a coffee shop for some sweet treats.

The castle is open to visitors every day throughout the summer months until about 2pm and entry is free. It is always wise to check first as it can often be closed for restoration work. Parking is a problem close to the castle and it is better to park in the village below and take the ten minute stroll upwards.

🌐 History & Folklore Museum of Argostoli

Ilia Zervou Str. 12, Argostoli, Kefalonia

Tel: +30 22850 22725

www.corgialenios.gr/

The museum shows elements of the island's history over a four century period. There are exhibits from the very first indication of life on Kefalonia as well as many artefacts from the Mycenaean Period. The folklore traditions of the

KEFALONIA TRAVEL GUIDE

island can clearly be seen in the displays of costumes, handmade utensils, carvings, jewellery and other everyday items.

There are 3000 photos of the island before and after various earthquakes showing just how devastating these natural disasters can be. Many of the photocopies of historical documents are available in English and Italian as well as Greek and a bedroom reconstruction shows how life was in times gone by.

The Folklore Museum is open Tuesday to Sunday from 8.30am to 3pm. If you have time the Koryalenios Library is in the same building as the museum and with 53,000 volumes is one of the largest libraries in Greece.

🌍 Koutavos Lagoon

Argostoli Bay

Kefalonia

Once swampland and impenetrable marshes the Koutavos Lagoon is now a super nature reserve where visitors can walk or cycle along from the harbour and follow the path round the lagoon. There are beautiful eucalyptus trees offering welcome shade from the sun as you make your way around and in the centre of the lagoon is a private island were the waterfowl nest and feed.

The lagoon is a natural stopping place for many migratory birds as they wing their way southwards for winter to parts of Europe and Africa. Loggerhead sea turtles can be seen but sadly numbers are declining as buildings and tourism encroach on their home that once was a swamp with nothing by malaria and mosquitoes.

Many organisations are keeping watch on the mating and breeding habits of the turtle both in the lagoon and at the Mounda beach.breeding ground to assess the situation of the population.

🌐 Three Island Cruise

There are several different boats that offer the cruise round the three islands and they all leave from the port at Agia Efimia. The itineraries are all fairly similar as the boats head north towards Lefkas passing the pretty cave of Papa Nicolas.

Then it is onward to one of the prettiest of the Ionian Islands, Meganissi. Some trips offer the chance to climb

KEFALONIA TRAVEL GUIDE

the 180 steps at Spartochori on this island from where there are simply breathtaking views across the forested slopes and beyond.

After that there is time to cruise around Skorpios Island, the favourite island of Aristotle Onassis and learn a little about the man and the history of the place he loved so much. Onassis bought the island in 1962 for a reputed sum of around £10,000 and this is where the shipping magnate married Jackie Kennedy in 1968.

The beautiful beach at Nidri is the next stop for lunch and a spot of swimming before heading back to Kefalonia.

Trip prices start at €35 for adults with reductions for children.

KEFALONIA TRAVEL GUIDE

🌐 Skala Beach & Town

Kefalonia

Skala is a great place to spend a day. Located right on the southeastern tip of Kefalonia the beaches with their golden sand go on forever, gently lapped by the Ionian Sea. The beach near the town has everything you need with sun beds, parasols, shops, tavernas and restaurants. For something a little quieter walk along the beach backed with pine trees until you find your own piece of paradise.

For the more adventurous there is a watersports and water ski club that has the latest kit for exhilarating rides across the water. You can take boat tours to Poros or to Katelios where there are some excellent fish restaurants.

KEFALONIA TRAVEL GUIDE

For walkers and hikers there are woodlands and open spaces for exploring at a gentle pace. Wander through olive groves and you will see impressive mosaic floors left behind by the Romans. The Roman villa with its magnificent tiled floors is open Tuesday to Sunday 9am to 3pm, entrance is free.

The town of Skala was destroyed during the 1953 earthquake and the majority of the buildings are quite modern. There are many old ruins around the town that can be explored.

KEFALONIA TRAVEL GUIDE

KEFALONIA TRAVEL GUIDE

Budget Tips

 Accommodation

Asta la Vista Mezonetes by the Sea

Pesádha

Kefalonia

Tel: +30 2671 025300

This hotel is just a very short walk to the beach and is ideal for couples, families or groups. The pretty terrace has great views to Mount Ainos as well as across the Ionian Sea and there is a small taverna close by which is ideal for breakfast and light snacks.

There is a 24 hour reception, luggage storage and a washing machine for guests to use. The rooms all have cable TV, hairdryers and air-conditioning. Asta la Vista Mezonetes by the Sea is disabled friendly and children and pets are welcome.

All the accommodation is self-catering and the apartments are fully equipped. A bed in a four-bedded apartment with a shared bathroom is just €25 per person per night in the middle of August.

Dioni Studios & Apartments

Poros,

Kefalonia 28086

Tel: +30 2674 073061

www.dioni.gr/

Only a short stroll from the sea these family run apartments offer excellent service and a friendly

KEFALONIA TRAVEL GUIDE

atmosphere. There are small beaches and rugged rocks to explore and if you fancy a boat ride to one of the other islands the port is nearby.

Dioni offers car parking, Wifi, 24 hour reception, a bar and a café. Breakfast isn't included but can be ordered at an extra cost.

All the studios and apartments are fully equipped with satellite TV, air-conditioning, dining area, hairdryer and ensuite facilities. The studios are great for two or three people while the apartments can sleep up to six people.

Sheets and towels are included and prices start from just €15 per person per night.

Alexatos Studios & Apartments

Artemidos 10

Agia Efimia

Kefalonia 28081

Tel: +30 2674 061524

These centrally located apartments and studios are a great place to stay with easy access. Situated in the north of the island and only ten minutes from Myrtos Beach you will get a friendly welcome and brilliant service.

The staff at Alexatos can also arrange hiking tours, riding or cycling, scuba diving and a whole host of other activities. There is a supermarket very close by where all the necessary provisions can be bought. Numerous tavernas are within walking distance so there is no excuse for not trying a glass of ouzo or two.

There are 15 rooms to choose from sleeping between 2 and 5 people. All the rooms are ensuite and prices start at €12.50 per person per night self-catering.

Star Villas Apartments

Agia Efimia, Kefalonia 28081

Tel: +30 26740 61519

www.starvillas.gr/

You can nearly fall out of bed and reach the sparkling blue sea from the Star Villa complex.

These newly built and spacious apartments are in Agia Efimia and are all self-catering.

KEFALONIA TRAVEL GUIDE

There is Wifi and wide selection of books to borrow. Each apartment has a modern and fully-equipped kitchen, lounge and a private bathroom. There is a selection of apartments to choose from with one, two or three bedrooms.

Prices start from just €13 per person per night.

Ventura Rooms

Main Street

Lassi, Kefalonia

Tel +30 2671 025019

With breathtaking views over the Ionian Sea these studios are family run and offer a personalised service for guests including airport transfers if required. There are beautiful gardens to relax in and sun-loungers for a quick snooze in the sun.

Ventura Rooms are only a short walk to the beach in one direction and into Lassi the other way where tavernas offer a selection of Greek specialities.

The studios all sleep two people and are well-furnished with modern bathrooms, a kitchenette and a private terrace with views.

A double or twin room starts at €36 per room per night.

 Restaurants, Cafés & Bars

Acropolis

Svoronata

Kefalonia

KEFALONIA TRAVEL GUIDE

Tel: +30 6979 760937

This restaurant is a favourite of many returning holidaymakers to Kefalonia which must say something about the food and service. With the freshest of produce available on the island prepared into interesting local and international dishes diners won't be disappointed.

The restaurant is bright and spacious with a pretty terrace for sitting outside and several times a week, depending on season, there is traditional Greek music. Sit back with a glass of Robola and listen to the mandolin, squeeze box and fiddle. If you fancy a dance try joining in the zonaratikos and impress your friends and family by imitating the fancy twists and turns of the dancers.

The Acropolis is open every evening from 5.30pm.

Kaliva

Skala

Kefalonia

Tel: +30 26710 83238

What would a holiday to a Greek island be without a spot of Zorba dancing and some plate smashing? Boring probably; so for a good night's fun and a lively atmosphere go to Skala for some great food and fantastic friendly service.

There is a selection of mezes to try and the main course of Greek klefitko is a very popular dish. This delicious mixture of succulent lamb cooked in foil with herbs and garlic just has to be tried. There are excellent salads as well and plenty of feta cheese and wine to share.

KEFALONIA TRAVEL GUIDE

The show starts around 9pm but do check before you make a special journey there. It can get very busy in the main season so may be worth calling ahead to book a table. The restaurant opens for breakfast, including a superb full English, as well as in the evenings. There is a daily specials board and free Wifi.

Taverna To Pefko

Fiskardo Road

Anti Pata

Kefalonia

This is a roadside restaurant where only the plastic awnings separate your table from the traffic but the food is fantastic. It is on the road to Fiskardo and this unpretentious restaurant is a refreshing change from the often crowded and noisy places to eat in the towns.

The food is simple Greek fare and all homemade. Try the pork souvlaki and fried courgettes or grilled haloumi cheese and hummus all washed down with some chilled Alfa beer

Polyphemus

Stavros

Ithaca

Kefalonia

Tel: +30 2674 031794

www.polyphemusithaca.com/

For a meal out with a difference take a ride over to the island of Ithaca and walk up the rather steep hill to the village of Stavros. Surrounded by a leafy garden strung with coloured lanterns is Polyphemus. This is a restaurant that has become a firm favourite with many visitors to the island.

Everywhere the walls are covered with pictures of Che Guevera and the chef Lazarus is well known for his wonderful cooking. The little tables and chairs are scattered in the olive grove and his Swiss wife will really make you feel at home. It is worth the effort to get there and they speak several languages between them, including English.

There are delights to try like sun-dried octopus, bream with currants and herbs and cheesy pitta bread. There is an excellent vegetarian selection to be enjoyed as well in the setting of this old Venetian building built in 1923.

Tselentis

Plateia Kavadia 39

Fiskardo 28084

Tel: +30 267 404 1344

This great restaurant is set back slightly from the harbour so doesn't charge exorbitant harbour view prices. The food is just as excellent though as at the sea front venues. Blue cheese salad and great pasta along with the freshest of fish are on the menu and always delicious.

The restaurant is run but a husband and wife team who will happily advise you on the dishes and let you have portions to share if you wish.

Tselentis is in a beautiful and historical house that has been owned by the family since 1893 and started as a small café. They are open for brunch, dinners and after hours.

🌐 Shopping

Most of the shops on the island open around 9am and close again at 2pm. Some will reopen at 5pm on Tuesdays, Thursdays and Fridays. Very few open on Sunday.

Down the Rabbit Hole

Kabanas Square

Argostoli

Kefalonia, 28100

Tel: +30 6946 259761

www.catharticchaos.co.uk

KEFALONIA TRAVEL GUIDE

If you want to find a unique piece of art or jewellery this is definitely the place to go. Everything in the shop is designed and made by the owner, Karen, who will happily make suggestions or even make an individual piece to your taste.

There are quirky animals and pieces inspired by gothic and Victorian times as well as many others at prices to suit all pockets.

Pantazatos Supermarket & Delicatessen

Antoni Tritsi 71

Argostoli

Tel: +30 26710 22513

With its bright yellow façade this supermarket is hard to miss on the Argostoli seafront. Starting out in life as a cheese shop it has grown into a delightful emporium of groceries and other everyday items. They still make all their own cheeses and yogurts as well a stocking favourite English brands like Heinz and cheddar cheese.

Robola Cooperative Factory Shop

Argostoli Harbour

Tel: +30 26710 86301

www.robola.gr/

Robola wine is the wine of Kefalonia and can be distinguished from others as the bottles are dressed in a smart hessian jacket with a gold medal around the neck. This dry white wine is only produced on Kefalonia from the grape of the same name and is not exported anywhere else.

There are other wines to choose from in the shop, either by the bottle or in bulk in glass flagons which are great for parties!

To stock up with some local Robola wine the shop is open Monday to Saturday 9am to 1.30pm and Tuesday, Thursday and Friday evenings 5pm to 8.30pm.

G G Garbis

24 Lithostroto Street

Argostoli

Tel: +30 26710 23164

www.garbis.gr

KEFALONIA TRAVEL GUIDE

This is a long-established business on the pretty island of Kefalonia and they use a selection of precious metals and fine stones to make a variety of jewellery. There is a collection of jewellery on display that was used in the film Captain Corelli's Mandolin and replicas are available to buy in yellow and white gold.

Another range of jewellery that is very popular features the Olive Branch design. This was made to commemorate the Olympic Games in Athens in 2004 and there are silver and gold pieces to choose from.

Look out as well for the lucky Year Charms in Sterling Silver and 14K Gold and maybe the next year will be full of fortune for you. There are also some beautifully handmade replicas of old Kefalonian coins available as key rings or charms.

Olive Press Gift Shop

Lithostroto

Argostoli

Kefalonia.

Tel: +30 26710 2662

Recommended as one of the best places on the island for gifts and souvenirs the shop is opposite St. Spridon's church in Lithostroto. The owner, Pauline, has a talent for making her window look attractive and the enticing displays just cannot be walked past without going into the shop to investigate further.

The gifts change to reflect the seasons and as well as a super selection of souvenirs there is beautiful jewellery in art deco style and in the many tones of amber. It is a

KEFALONIA TRAVEL GUIDE

great place to visit and if you are buying items as presents the staff will wrap them free of charge for you.

KEFALONIA TRAVEL GUIDE

Know Before You Go

Entry Requirements

By virtue of the Schengen agreement, travellers from other countries in the European Union do not need a visa when visiting Greece. Additionally visitors from certain countries such as Canada, Japan, Israel, Australia, Argentina, Monaco, Andorra, Brazil, Brunei, Chile, Costa Rica, Croatia, Honduras, Guatemala, El Salvador, Nicaragua, Paraguay, Panama, San Marino, Singapore, South Korea, Uruguay, New Zealand and the Vatican State do not need visas if their stay in Greece does not exceed 90 days in a six month period. In the case of travellers from the USA, entry requirements will depend on the type of passport held. While visitors with a normal blue tourist passport will be able to enter the USA without a visa, holders of red official or black diplomatic passports must apply for a Schengen visa prior to departure and will face deportation if attempting to enter Greece without the necessary documentation.

🌍 Health Insurance

Citizens of other EU countries as well as residents from Switzerland, Norway, Iceland, Liechtenstein and the UK are covered for health care in Greece with the European Health Insurance Card (EHIC), which can be applied for free of charge. If you need a Schengen visa for your stay in Greece, you will also be required to obtain proof of health insurance for the duration of your stay (that offers at least €37,500 coverage), as part of your visa application. Visitors from Canada or the USA should check whether their regular health insurance covers travel and arrange for extended health insurance if required.

🌍 Travelling with Pets

Greece participates in the Pet Travel Scheme (PETS) which allows UK residents to travel with their pets without requiring quarantine upon re-entry. Pets travelling between different countries in the EU will need to be accompanied by a valid pet passport, which can be obtained from any licensed veterinarian in the EU. The animal will have to be microchipped and up to date on rabies vaccinations. To visit Greece, your pet will need to be accompanied by a good health certificate issued by a vet no more than ten days prior to your intended departure. The certificate must be in both English and Greek. You should also have a rabies vaccination certificate no less than 30 days and no more than 12 months old. If travelling from a high rabies country, a blood titer test will need to be submitted three months prior to your travel plans. Your animal's microchip should be non-encrypted and compliant with a 15 digit ISO 11784/11785 number (or alternatively you will need to have your own scanner handy.) You will be required to make a declaration of non-commercial travel. If returning to the USA with a pet you adopted in Greece, your pet will need to be vaccinated against rabies at least 30 days prior to entry into the USA.

Airports

Athens International Airport (ATH) is the busiest airport in Greece. Located about 20km east of the city center, it is the main airport servicing Athens and the region of Attica. **Heraklion International Airport** (HER) is located on the island of Crete, about 5km east of the city of Heraklion. It is the second busiest airport in Greece. **Thessaloniki International Airport** (SKG), also known as Makedonia International Airport, provides access to Khalkidhiki, the region of Macedonia and the northern part of Greece. It is located in Mikra and serves Thessaloniki, the second largest city in Greece. **Rhodes International Airport** (RHO) is located on the western side of the island Rhodes. It is the 4th busiest airport in Greece, providing regular connections to Athens. **Corfu International Airport** (CFU) is located on the island of Corfu, about 2km south of Corfu City. **Mykonos Island National Airport** (JMK) about 4km from Mykonos Town and **Santorini National Airport** (JTR), provide seasonal connections to the Cyclades at the peak of the summer holidays.

🌐 Airlines

Olympic Airlines, the national flag carrier of Greece for more than 50 years, ceased operation in 2009 due to bankruptcy. From the privatization of its assets, a regional airline, Olympic Air, was formed. Ellinair is a small Greek airline that was established in 2013 and provides regional connections between Athens and Thessaloniki as well as regular flights to Russia, Latvia and the Ukraine. Minoan Air is a small airline based in Heraklion on the island of Crete. It provides connections to Kos and Rhodes, as well as seasonal flights to Santorini and Mytilene. Sky Express is also headquartered in Crete and provides regional connections to 18 Greek destinations. Another Greek airline based in Crete, Bluebird Airways, flies to the Greek destinations of Araxos, Corfu, Kos and Rhodes as well as destinations in Israel, Russia and Turkey.

Athens International Airport serves as a main hub for Aegean Airlines as well as Olympic Air. Olympic Air also uses Rhodes International Airport as a secondary hub. Heraklion

KEFALONIA TRAVEL GUIDE

International Airport serves as a hub for Bluebird Airways Minoan Air and Sky Express. It is also a focus city for Aegean Airlines. Thessaloniki International Airport serves as a hub for Aegean Airlines, Astra Airlines, Ellinair and Ryanair.

🌐 Currency

The currency of Greece is the Euro. It is issued in notes in denominations of €500, €200, €100, €50, €20, €10 and €5. Coins are issued in denominations of €2, €1, 50c, 20c, 10c, 5c, 2c and 1c.

🌐 Banking & ATMs

You will find ATMs in the larger centers of Greece, although smaller towns may only have a single ATM machine. Greek ATMs are configured for four-digit PIN numbers - make sure your card is compliant before leaving home. However, the financial crisis has introduced an added complication. While daily limits imposed on Greek citizens do not apply to tourists visiting the country, you may encounter ATMs that have run out of cash or banks that are reluctant to exchange pounds for euros. The limits imposed on Greeks will also make it difficult for shop owners to provide change for cash sales. To be on the safe side, consider taking cash in smaller denominations. Do

KEFALONIA TRAVEL GUIDE

remember to advise your bank of your travel plans before leaving home.

🌐 Credit Cards

The Credit Cards most widely used in Greece are MasterCard and Visa, although American Express is also accepted at more touristy centers. While shops and many hotels accept credit cards, most restaurant options will be limited to cash. Credit card machines in Greece are configured for chip-and-pin type credit cards and you may run into trouble with an older magnetic strip credit card. Greece also has representatives of Western Union, for international money transfers.

🌐 Reclaiming VAT

If you are not from the European Union, you can claim back VAT (Value Added Tax) paid on your purchases in Greece. The VAT rate in Greece is 23 percent, although it varies on certain types of goods and you will qualify for a refund on goods of €120 and over. To reclaim, you must ask the merchant to fill in a refund voucher. You will be asked to show your passport. Make sure that the form is completed and attach your sales slip to the form. The goods must be inspected at the place where you leave the European Union. Here, the necessary documentation will be processed. Your refund will only be valid for items that are still unused at your time of departure. If the merchant is affiliated to Global Refund or Premier Tax Free, you will be able to collect the refund from their offices at the airport in the currency of your choice. A 4 percent service charge will be levied. Alternatively, you could ask for a refund on your credit card or contact the retailer directly, once you have returned home.

Tipping Policy

At the hotel, tip the porter €1 per bag and the housekeeper €1 per day. At restaurants, you should tip between 5 and 10 percent of the bill, depending on its size. Bear in mind that the service or cover charge on your restaurant bill (usually around €1) is for the table's bread and water. It is customary to tip tour guides in Greece. For a group tour, between €2 and €5 per person is fair. For private tours, €20 per person is the expected rate. On a yacht cruise, tip the captain or skipper between 5 and 15 percent (in a closed envelope) for him to distribute amongst crew members. With taxi drivers, it is customary to round off the amount or to tip between 5 and 10 percent. If you employed a private driver, tip him €20 per day.

🌐 Mobile Phones

Most EU countries, including Greece uses the GSM mobile service. This means that most UK phones and some US and Canadian phones and mobile devices will work in Greece. However, phones using the CDMA network will not be compatible. While you could check with your service provider about coverage before you leave, using your own service in roaming mode will involve additional costs. The alternative is to purchase a Greek SIM card to use during your stay in Greece. Greece has three mobile networks. They are Cosmote, Vodafone and Wind. Of the three networks, Wind is the most economic, but offers the lowest coverage. With each network, you can choose between packages that offer data only or a mixture of voice, text and data. A basic Cosmote SIM with no credit can be purchased for €5, but you will want to look at some of the available package deals as well. Vodafone offers a starter package that includes 2 GB data that can be ordered online for €15, but will cost €20 in store. At Wind you have the choice of a free SIM with top-up cards from €10 or a SIM for €5. They also offer mobile broadband. As per legislation that came into effect in 2009, all Greek SIM cards must be registered before they can be activated. This can only be done in person and you will need to show some form of identification, such as a passport. You can recharge your airtime by buying scratch cards or electronically from ATMs, certain vendors or online with a debit or credit card.

Dialling Code

The international dialling code for Greece is +30.

Emergency numbers

General Emergencies: 112

Police: 100

Fire Brigade: 199

Emergency Medical Service: 166

Coast Guard: 108

Emergency Social Assistance: 197

Tourist Police: 171

MasterCard: 00 800 11 887 0303

Visa: 00 800 11 638 0304

Public Holidays

1 January: New Year's Day

6 January: Day of the Epiphany

February/March: Orthodox Ash Monday

25 March: Independence Day

April (variable): Orthodox Good Friday

KEFALONIA TRAVEL GUIDE

April (variable): Orthodox Easter Sunday

April (variable): Orthodox Easter Monday

1 May: Labour Day

May/June: Orthodox Pentecost

May/June: Orthodox Whit Monday

15 August: Assumption Day

28 October: Ochi Day (Oxi Day/Ohi Day)

25 December: Christmas Day

26 December: Second Christmas Day

Time Zone

Greece falls in the Eastern European Time Zone. This can be calculated (from the end of October to the end of March) as follows: Greenwich Mean Time/Coordinated Universal Time (GMT/UTC) +2; Eastern Standard Time (North America) -6; Pacific Standard Time (North America) -9.

Daylight Savings Time

Clocks are set forward one hour on the last Sunday of March and set back one hour on the last Sunday of October for Daylight Savings Time.

🌐 School Holidays

The academic year begins in the second week of September and ends in mid June. The summer holiday is from mid June to the first third of September. There are short breaks between Christmas and New Year and also around Easter.

🌐 Trading Hours

In Greece, trading hours vary according to the type of business. You can expect supermarkets to be open from 8am to 8pm on weekdays and until 6pm on Saturdays. Most other shops are open between 9am and 1pm and then again for a late session between 6pm and 9pm. The hours from 1.30pm to 5.30pm are for lunch and siesta, especially in the summer months. Post Offices are open from 8am to 8pm on weekdays and from 8am to 2pm on Saturdays. Shops that cater for tourists may be open until 11pm, especially during the peak tourist season. Pharmacies conform to normal shopping hours, but are usually closed on Saturdays.

🌐 Driving Laws

Greeks drive on the right hand side of the road. A driver's licence from any of the European Union member countries is valid in Greece, but visitors from non-EU countries should apply for an International Driver's License. The minimum driving age in Greece is 18. You will need to have a Green Insurance certificate, also known as a Green Card to cover third party liability and your vehicle needs standard safety gear such as warning triangles, a first aid kit and fire extinguisher. Your vehicle also needs to have headlamp deflectors. The speed limit in Greece is 130km per hour on freeways and 50km an hour on urban roads. The alcohol limit in Greece is under 0.5 g/l. Children under the age of 10 are not allowed to ride in the front seat. It is illegal to use your mobile phone while driving.

Smoking Laws

Greece is the European country with the highest tobacco consumption rate. As a result, the population has been very tolerant of smoking, even with the introduction of anti-smoking legislation. In fact, business owners have appealed against various forms of anti-smoking laws, arguing that they are bad for business. Smoking in public places has been banned since 2010, but the law provides for bars, taverns, casinos, night clubs and betting shops to create a designated smoking area. It is also illegal to smoke in your car, if in the company of a minor child.

Drinking Laws

The legal drinking age in Greece is 18. Although Greece has a culture of social drinking, bars and night clubs may state that alcohol will not be served to under 18s or even, in the case of certain cruise tours, under 21s. Alcohol can be bought from supermarkets and even fast food outlets.

Electricity

Electricity: 230 volts

Frequency: 50 Hz

Greek electricity sockets use the Type F plugs, which feature two round pins or prongs. They are also compatible with Type C and Type E plugs. If travelling from the USA, you will need a power converter or transformer to convert the voltage from 230 to 110, to avoid damage to your appliances. The latest models of many laptops, camcorders, mobile phones and digital cameras are dual-voltage with a built in converter.

Tourist Information (TI)

There are three National Tourist Offices in the city of Athens where you can pick up maps of the city, as well as time tables for the Greek bus, train and ferry services. They are located at

Athens Eleftherios Venizelos Airport, in the Athens Center at 26A Amalias Avenue and 7 Tsoha Street.

🌍 Food & Drink

Greek cuisine relies heavily on the use of olive oil (and olives), cheese and aubergines (or eggplant). Beef is rare, but there are plenty of lamb and pork dishes to make up for it. One of the most popular Greek dishes is moussaka, a casserole consisting of layers of eggplant and spiced mince. Try the baked pasta dish, pastitsio or if you like meat stews, do make sure that you try stifado as well. With an abundance of seafood available, don't forget to enjoy the abundance of grilled fish and octopus. A course of small meze dishes is often served as appetizer or to accompany a round of drinks. The standard meze favorites include tzatziki (a dip of yoghurt and cucumber), hummus (made of chickpea), dolmades, keftedes, olives, feta cheese and taramasalata (a fish roe dip), usually served with pita or flatbread. Another delicious appetizer is saganaki, or fried cheese, often made with halloumi, kefalotyri, graviera, kefalograviera or feta. Graviera, which is a native product of Crete, is the second most popular cheese in Greece after feta. Fast and meaty snacks to enjoy on the go are souvlaki (meat skewers), kebabs or gyros - pitas filed with meat, French fries and smothered in tzatziki. Phyllo pastry is used for a variety of dishes, including the standard dessert of baklava and tiropitakia

KEFALONIA TRAVEL GUIDE

(or cheese pies). If you happen to find yourself on Mykonos, do make sure you sample kopanisti, a cheesy appetizer, a few slices of louza, the local salami and some amigthalota, to indulge your sweet tooth. Crete is a must for cheese lovers, where practically every village has its own distinctive varieties. Here you can also enjoy Askordoulakous or "mountain bulbs", lamb with stamnagathi or sfakia pies. For a taste of manouri - a cheese similar to feta with a creamier character - you need to be in Thessaly or Macedonia.

The most popular beers local beer in Greece is Mythos, although Amstel and Heineken are also available at most venues. Retsina is the type of wine most often associated with Greece, although its distinctive taste of resin is not all that popular with foreigners. Another popular drink is ouzo, a strong liquor with a minty taste that combines well with seafood. If visiting Epirus, Macedonia or Crete, to sample the local raki and tsipouro, which is served in small shot glasses. If you want to quench your thirst with something refreshing and non-alcoholic, try soumada, a Cretan beverage of almond and rose water.

 **Websites**

http://www.visitgreece.gr/

http://www.greeka.com/best-greece-destinations.htm

KEFALONIA TRAVEL GUIDE

http://www.greek-tourism.gr/

http://wikitravel.org/en/Greece

http://www.visit-ancient-greece.com/

http://www.greektravel.com/mainland.htm

Printed in Great Britain
by Amazon